STIG AND SPUD

Written by Gina Nuttall

Illustrated by Sarah Goodreau

Spud has lots of grub.
Rat gets all the grub!

2

Spud puffs.
He cannot grab Rat.

Spud is not fit.
Stig has a plan. She grins.

Stig gets Spud to jog up hills.

She gets him to swim in
the pond.

Spud skips on the spot.

Spud jumps and he is glad.

Spud has some grub.
Rat gets the grub!

But Spud is fit so he is quick.

Spud gets the grub back!